SIMPLY LEAP

Seven Lessons on Facing Fear and Enjoying the Crap out of Your Life

LAUREE OSTROFSKY

SIMPLY LEAP

Seven Lessons on Facing Fear and
Enjoying the Crap out of Your Life

LAUREE OSTROFSKY

Cover design by Rebecca Nolen
Author photo by Sweet Alice Photography

Printed in the United States of America

ISBN Paperback: 978-1539117612

[TO MY FAMILY, WHO KNEW
I WAS A WRITER BEFORE I DID.]

Introduction

"You should write a book about reinventing yourself."

My dad said this to me after watching an episode of "Doctor Who." The television was silent after shutting off his DVR, a rare occurrence, and he stared out the living room windows onto the snowy lawn on that gray January afternoon.

He spoke as if in response to a conversation we were already having. Maybe in his mind we were. The faraway look on his face meant he was somewhere else, with thoughts buzzing faster than either of us could keep up. I assume Einstein had those looks often.

It was how I knew he was serious. A moment later his face lit up and his eyes turned back to me:

"This is perfect. You could talk about what you've done. It's a bestseller."

I shrugged and laughed, searching my own mind for what this might mean, and then looked out at the lawn, too.

Twenty-four hours later, I began writing.

In 2003 I was in a good-enough career, in a good-enough relationship, and living a good-enough A-student life. I could have kept doing it all forever. Trying hard to be who I thought others needed and wanted. Seeking the gold stars that came easily in third grade but in the real world, to my disappointment, weren't as clear-cut to achieve. Wanting praise from my family, bosses, even my dentist, to replace how good it felt to see 'Great job!' in red pen on my report cards. Believing that if others thought I was on the right track, they must be right.

Then suddenly, good-enough wasn't good enough anymore.

With that realization, everything else began to shift. I propelled myself beyond the life of should's and have-to's into the one waiting for me.

I took a six-week sabbatical traveling through Europe to be more creative without leaving my corporate job, and then I left my job a year later. I found my life purpose while lying in a hospital bed. I went to art school and rekindled my love of nature and storytelling. I built a business helping successful-on-paper A-students like myself figure out what they really want to be doing. I ended a major romantic relationship (twice). I sold or gave away nearly all of my belongings (twice). I traveled to twelve countries (and counting). I moved to Manhattan, then Washington, D.C., and then back to my childhood home, that very living room, in the Hudson Valley of Upstate New York. I spoke in front of hundreds of people while shaking in fear. I wrote a book and toured the country for six months. I hugged a mayor and a TV weatherman, and found my calling from Maya Angelou. I received 300 valentines.

I will not lie. I still love gold stars. I have also tripped over the occasional curb and smacked into concrete walls, many of my own making. As tough as they seemed at the time, in retrospect they appear part of the plan.

My life went from good-enough to more amazing than I could ever have imagined.

How?

When I look back at my reinventions, and how I help clients do the same, there is a pattern: Seven lessons that change first how you see your life and then change your life itself.

I won't lie about this either: Some people stop. I did mention a concrete wall or two; it can get uncomfortable, scary. Walls do exist, but they are <u>all</u> surmountable.

How I simply leaped into a life I love full of people I'm honored to call my friends and family was by taking one lesson at a time.

I had to understand better what I really wanted, so when great things showed up on my doorstep I could recognize they were meant for me.

I had to see how much I already had, and be grateful for it.

I had to ask for help, and accept it.

I had to shift old beliefs weighing me down that just weren't true, like I have to work hard, love has to be earned, and my life should look like everyone else's. *You mean it doesn't?*

I had to recognize my own progress.

I had to believe delightful surprises and perfectly-timed serendipities were possible, even when I couldn't see them yet, because then they happened.

You can do all of those things, too.

In fact, if you're like some of my favorite clients who I describe in this book, you'll probably be better at it than I am. You know the saying about the student becoming the teacher? That's the case with every one of them.

They have changed careers, started businesses, remade their good-enough jobs into great ones, moved cross-country or abroad, had the marriages-babies-sabbaticals of their dreams, literally and figuratively climbed mountains, and loved the crap out of their lives. Impromptu dance parties included.

It was an honor to be with them for these milestones, and to be with you now as you embark on your own.

Are you ready to make some magic?

CHAPTER 1

Be Ready

[Be ready]

I'm fully prepared for you not to make it past this point in the book.

How's that for an opening?

Do you remember Willy Wonka (I'm talking Gene Wilder, not Johnny Depp) and how it wasn't enough to have the golden ticket or not to get caught in an unfortunate candy accident? Charlie still had to show he was ready and able to receive the enormous gift he was about to be given.

That's what I'm asking from you now.

You need to put in the effort in order to get the results. Much of this isn't hard. Some of it is. Which parts are tough are different for every person. That's why I'm here for the whole ride, so if or when there is a bump in the road you know where to find me.

Riding shotgun.

Hanging just off camera, jumping up and down with pompoms.

Lesson 1 is to Be Ready.

What do you need to do in order to Be Ready?

You need to recognize that where you are now is good-enough, maybe even great – but there is more out there that is meant for you.

You need to know you deserve a happier, healthier, more interesting, more fun, more adventurous, more fulfilling life than the one you have right now. Maybe you recognize you're living someone else's life; the one you (or your parents, significant other or best friend) think you *should* be living, not the one that feels right for you.

You also need to take a good look around, because your life won't look the same again. It can be sad to admit that. Some of the people in your life will fall away to make room for the new you and for the new people who will support you in ways the others had a hard time doing.

And, it's not just people. You may shed your job, your city, or in my case (twice) most of your belongings, things that suddenly feel too small or never fit to begin with. Maybe it's already started to happen. Either way, you can Be Ready for it. Letting go of the parts of your life that don't feel like the real you is a loving side effect of your growth.

What really slips away is the belief that you ever have to work hard to gain respect, attention and love again - including from yourself.

This is about *Simply* Leaping, which means *you allowing it to be simple.* Allowing yourself to have what you want, allowing your life to look the way you dreamed, and allowing people to respect and love you for yourself. Not because you worked hard, but because you deserved it all along. You're fantastic. This means believing you're fantastic; life tends to treat you how you treat yourself.

...

Being Ready is also really, really exciting.

Imagining the innumerable ways your life will change in the coming months can put a gigantic spring in your step.

"Not long now, and I'm outta here!"

"Watch out world. Something wonderful is about to happen!"

It's true.

Opening yourself up to the change that is about to happen – even and especially when you don't know what that change is yet – is vital to your ability to seize opportunities that land in your lap.

They are already here. Without doing anything different, serendipity, luck, and chance are in your favor in every moment of every day.

Great things happen to people who are looking for them.

Read that again. Fantastical things beyond your imagination happen when you are willing and able to see them.

It's like wearing night vision goggles. Without them, you're stuck in the dark reaching out for nearby furniture, trying not the stub your toe. With them, you realize this whole time you've been standing in front of a table filled with beautifully wrapped gifts, all labeled with your name.

Nothing has changed in the scenario except your ability to see. That is true in your life, too. Be Ready to see what has been right in front of you the whole time, including helpful people, new ideas, and the career of your dreams.

Which brings me to...

You say you want something. Now imagine yourself actually getting it.

Those are two very different steps. Wanting something can be easy. We've wanted things since we were born. Back then, uncontrollable crying forced everyone in our vicinity to figure out what they could do so we would be content again.

It's a shame it doesn't work that way anymore. Now you're the only one searching for what will satisfy your hunger, soothe your discomfort.

Good thing you are as powerful as you are. Piece of cake...to go with all of those presents.

I'm not kidding, either. Nearly every client I have ever worked with at some point has uttered, "You'll never guess what happened..."

I am usually as delighted as they are about what it was, but rarely am I caught off guard. Amazing things happen when you expect they will, and when you are actively looking for them.

Which is why one of the first things I ask new clients is what they will do when what they want arrives.

You would think this would be a simple question to answer, but it's not.

I help clients get what they want. It's a fact. It's also a fact that most of them have NO IDEA what to do when they get it.

There are two main reactions when something they've really wanted comes together faster and easier than they thought it would:

1. They can be shocked: "I got what I wanted? Really? I figured this would be harder."

2. Or, they can freak out: "What I want arrived! It's really here! What do I do now?!"

That's why you need to Be Ready.

Spend time imagining your new and wonderful life. Even if you don't know where you'll be, what you'll be doing, or who else will be there. You don't have to know any of those things just yet. Imagine yourself happy. Get really clear about what being happy feels like for you. Where you feel it in your body. Does it radiate out of you? Does it have a color? Is there a sound that goes with it?

Connect to that feeling regularly, daily, and then ask yourself:

What will I do when I feel this way all the time?

If you're not sure, no worries. Most of us don't know the answer when asked the first time. Keep feeling what it feels like to be happy...living debt-free, not having to go to that crappy office job anymore, being in a loving relationship...whatever a great life is like for you.

Ask yourself the question again and again until you feel your way to the answer.

- I will smile every day.

- I will know I can do anything I want. This milestone will be my proof, and I will not doubt myself again.

- I will set up an automatic withdrawal every month to go into a Roth-IRA. (Specific actions are helpful, too.)

Once you have your answers, you'll be more ready than many of my clients and almost everyone else. Congratulations on starting!

As you continue to read this book, notice:

What seems like a natural next step for you, and what feels completely out of reach?

Out of reach doesn't mean impossible. It may mean that it is out of your comfort zone, and you need an extra push. That's helpful information. It can encourage you to find moral support, or to decide to just go for it because fear won't get in your way. This would be your "*I'm scared & doing it anyway*" moment. (If you don't know the reference, that's the name of my first book, a story about facing my own fears and the life-affirming and love-filled things that happened as a result.)

Alternatively, it can mean you need to spend more time right where you are. That is a fine decision to make; I've done it more times than I can count. My story seems put-together because you weren't living with me through the moments when I didn't know how it would work out, the 3:00 a.m. what-if's while staring at the ceiling in the middle of the night. The unending questions I posed to good friends who reassured me I was on the right track, even when sometimes they weren't sure either. Change takes time, especially the kind of fulfilling life and career change you so richly deserve. Hanging out in one of the lessons in this book for a while until you feel ready is what all the pros do, so bonus points if you decide to take that route at some point.

Just beware of the voice that is scared and telling you to do nothing or turn back. During our work together, you will hear that voice a few times and it will sound very convincing.

"I can't go any further."

"This isn't right for me."

"I've never been here before. I don't feel safe."

"I want to go back to what's familiar, what I know."

Being Ready is giving yourself time to get your bearings, not backing off because you're scared.

You know yourself well enough to determine which of these is happening, as it is happening. I trust you and your instincts.

If you're ever not sure which it is, keep doing what makes you uncomfortable and see what happens. If it's fear, it will subside or yell louder, and you'll be onto it by then. If it's the need to slow down and be where you are, you will feel sluggish and tired as you keep moving forward. You might feel like you missed something, and you probably have. Go back and take a load off (naps help), knowing you are right where you are supposed to be, and then try again a little later.

...

Where does that leave us?

You have all the tools you need to Be Ready. Walk yourself through this chapter checking to see if everything I'm describing sounds reasonable. Do you know what you want and how you will know when it arrives?

You better, because it's going to happen.

[CLIENT STORY: READY OR NOT!]

Sometimes clients are more ready than I am. Well I should say, sometimes clients astonish me with how fast they move, and how deeply they believe that anything and everything is possible. They are out of the gate while I'm still settling in, and then suddenly I'm running to keep up and wondering just how far they will take us both. One client in particular I've had the pleasure to work with during several of her mind-blowing leaps through the years.

We met over brunch with mutual friends, her bright, happy eyes beaming across the table. A couple months later she reached out. Ready. She had recently turned 30 and it made her think ahead to 40. She wanted to be content, fulfilled and confident about her life by then.

At the moment she felt the opposite. She wasn't sure if she wanted to stay at the corporation where she worked. She wasn't sure if she liked what she did, or if there was something better somewhere else. She wasn't sure if she and her husband wanted to have children. Most of all, she wasn't sure how one gets to "be sure" about any of it, but she knew she was ready to figure it out.

In our first session, we imagined her life ten years in the future. How peaceful and present she would feel knowing she was in the right place and implicitly trusting her choices. I often take new clients on an imaginary visit to their future selves, because it requires less figuring out when you know at some point you'll know all the answers!

Sounds a little meta, but it works. It did for this client. Meeting her future self meant she knew better where she was headed even if she still didn't know how she would get there. It confirmed even more what she wanted was possible – and as I learned quickly, when she is clear about her goal and knows others believe in it too, she is unstoppable.

What happened? She changed roles within her company to expand her skills and make more of a difference, she took leadership classes and joined a nonprofit board, she became a nurse while still at her corporate job, she took up rock climbing and orienteering, she moved to Singapore for a year and a half work assignment, she got divorced and sold her house, and she starting telling people she loved them. In fact, we end our calls with it and I can feel how much she means it every time.

By her 39th birthday she had reinvented nearly everything, or perhaps become more of who she was meant to be all along. Then she took an even more daring leap.

That story a little later.

...

For now, let's get back to you.

In this first chapter we looked at why Be Ready is so important to achieving what you want. We named some scary roadblocks that can get in the way and we laid the groundwork for your own mind-blowing leap with inspiration from one of my leap-iest of clients.

Finally, to help you get the most out of each lesson in this book, you'll see sample homework assignments throughout. Lessons stick when they are accompanied by doing, so give at least one of these a whirl or consider designing your own. Taking a step – no matter how small and no matter in what direction – gets you closer to your dreams.

Ready?

[HOMEWORK: BE READY]

- Take an honest look at your life. What's already working? What else do you wish were here – more money, time, love, appreciation?

- How will you know when what you want arrives? How will you feel? What will you say, think, do when your vision becomes a reality? It's going to happen. Now is the moment to Be Ready.

- Get really clear about what it feels like when you're scared and out of your comfort zone. Make a list of which kind words and tender actions help you feel better and able to keep moving. Having them now means you're ready when you need them later.

- Put on your night vision goggles and see all of the goodness around you. More is on the way!

CHAPTER 2

Enjoy the Crap out of Your Life

[Enjoy the crap out of your life]

Woo hoo! Dance party!

If you have never had an impromptu dance party in your kitchen while drinking wine, baking chocolate chip cookies, and wearing pajamas, this is a good time to start.

If you have, then you know how good it feels to do silly, fun things for no reason other than because you can. I once made myself a Wonder Woman crown and bracelets out of aluminum foil on a Sunday afternoon, because it made me laugh.

Other than a list of all the fun things you can do to be a kid again (which we will discuss in a minute), this chapter has a necessary purpose.

Put simply, if you aren't enjoying life now, you probably won't enjoy it when you reach your goal, either.

People withhold enjoyment from themselves constantly, like they are their own mean parents who won't let them have dessert until they finish all their vegetables or check everything off their to-do lists. They forget they are adults now and can do pretty much whatever they want. They don't need to be threatened into or out of anything.

Yes, that means you can have dessert any time you want. You don't have to prove you're deserving or have done enough. That may feel like utter anarchy in the beginning, but go with it. That's just the mean-parent part of you afraid of losing control. On the other side of really giving yourself permission to enjoy your life and do what you want to do when you want to do it, everything will balance out again.

Lesson 2 is to Enjoy the Crap out of Everything.

In the last chapter, I introduced the concept of getting ready for being happy. Imagine how good it will feel to reach your goals, and start feeling that way now. This chapter builds on that. Your challenge now is to enjoy the crap out of every aspect of your life, even the people who frustrate you and the chores languishing at the bottom of your to-do list.

First off, recognize if and how you're holding yourself back from fully enjoying your current life. You can list all the reasons why your life isn't great or perfect yet. Your boss who doesn't appreciate you, the bills you have to pay, a weekly schedule that doesn't feel like your own...None of those frustrating things need to change in order for you to be happy.

The only thing that needs to change is Y O U.

The person I was in 2013 would have hated me for saying that. I would have thought, "What the heck does that mean anyway? That's something woo-woo people who are completely together say to the rest of us who have shit to do."

Pot, Kettle, Black = Me. I get why you might feel that way. However, it's still true.

No matter what is happening, you have control over how you think and feel about it, how you talk about it, and what you do about it. The more empowered you feel, the bigger the shifts you will make.

Spend a minute thinking about what's not working in your life. Really feel that frustration and disappointment. It's valid.

Now, look even more closely at this situation that isn't going well. What is great about it? There is something fantastic about what isn't working. Look hard and find it. Why are you SO LUCKY that this is happening? Why is this proof that you are right where you are supposed to be?

When I do this, for instance, I imagine the person I'm having the most difficulty with and love the crap out of them in my mind. Turning the quirkiest characteristics in my loved ones into some of my favorite features about them. Why can't that be possible for everyone I meet?

This is a muscle you will develop over time. It may already be stronger than you think it is, or you may need to start with the three-pound barbells until you get used to this workout. No matter, if you keep at it you'll be a svelte bodybuilder of positivity before long. (I just wanted a reason to use the word, svelte, because I like the spelling.)

[SIDEBAR: FUN]

I covered the tougher part first; now it's time for pure fun. Hopefully easier to implement, maybe because you're a natural!

This is the moment to let your imagination run wild. Think back to when you were four or five years old — to your favorite game, your imaginary friend, or the knock-knock joke that always gave you a case of the giggles.

Spend time with the younger you, getting to know that kid again from your adult perspective. What would the younger you like best about your outfit today? What would fascinate them about your living room? See your life through their wide-open eyes.

You may have grown up, but that cute, precocious child is still inside and will lead us to the real fun.

How?

Make a list of at least ten things the Younger You wants to do. Your job, besides dutifully taking notes, is to do some or all of these things today, starting the moment you put down your pen.

This is the list from my younger self:

* Fly a kite.
* Blow bubbles in a glass of milk.
* Pick weeds and pretend they are flowers.
* Run barefoot everywhere.
* Make a fort out of blankets and couch cushions.
* Listen to a story read out loud.
* Fog up a mirror and draw a smiley face.
* Walk into a candy store and stare at brightly colored gumballs.
* Jump up and down on the bed.
* Write in magic marker.
* Sing in the shower.
* Sparkles. Sprinkles. Everywhere.

I'm writing this list in a cafe, and I just picked up a glass of water and blew bubbles into it for twenty seconds. Totally worth it.

What did you do?

The more time I spend with my younger self, the more I appreciate her resourcefulness and creativity. I'm proud of her – and that pride fills a deep reservoir the adult me can tap into. Even thinking about fun makes life better.

You're not getting off the hook, though; you still have to do these things, not just think about them. Do a few from your list today, and more tomorrow. If you don't think you have time to hang your head out of a passenger-side window, letting the air blow your hair, then hang your head out of the driver's side!

This may seem like it doesn't relate to the bigger goals you set as you began this book, but it does. Remember that your enjoyment of life <u>now</u> is directly proportional to your enjoyment of life after achieving what you want. There is no worthwhile reason to delay gratification.

In other words, playtime!

Hopefully, there is already a smile on your face.

If not, go ahead and give me a good one, even if you don't feel like it. Fake it and look around for something deserving that smile on your face. Scientific research says your brain can't tell the difference between a real smile and a fake one, and releases the same positive hormones either way.

Sometimes I smile while driving alone in the car just to start the positivity flowing. Try it!

[CLIENT STORY: THE MAGICAL COFFEE SHOP]

I love this client. I may have told her that, several times.

Before we started coaching a couple years ago, she was already well versed in affirmations, journaling, Brené Brown, and the power of positive thinking. We took what she was already doing, and used it to go after her blind spots.

She knew she had a great marriage, because of the open communication and fun they both shared. But she felt stagnant at work, as if the only way to be the creative, difference-making problem-solver she knew she could be would mean quitting her job and finding a workplace – and a boss – who valued her.

She may well do that someday, but where she ended up in the meantime rocks my socks. She is now internationally respected, using improvisation and other masterful creativity tools to solve big hairy problems within organizations, including higher education. And, she accomplished this without leaving her job.

I'll let her write the book about how she did that. I'm positive she will. For now, I'll cut to the part about the coffee shop.

She took very seriously the lesson to enjoy the crap out of everything – the sillier, the better.

To carve out time in her busy schedule, she blocked an hour on her calendar with the words, "Lauree will hate you if you do not honor this time!" She smirked whenever she saw it, which helped her commit to the break more often.

Her positive affirmations included a picture of Animal from "The Muppet Show" on her desk, and she instituted a secret word of the day similar to "Pee-wee's Playhouse," the late eighties Saturday morning television show. Whenever someone in her office would say a word that bugged her, such as "compensation," she would scream *AAAAHHHHHH* in her head and laugh to herself. During our next session, she would relay the story and we would scream and laugh together about it.

Bringing her full silly self to work changed how she felt while she was there, and as she enjoyed herself more, more opportunities came her way.

Around this time, she started having meetings in what she referred to as her Magical Coffee Shop, an actual café just down the street from her office building.

Though work and her boss were much better – or she felt much better about them – she still wanted a great new job offer. We imagined how it would take place in the coffee shop, so she would be excited every time she walked through its doors. The magic could happen today! From that moment on, when someone she would love to work with approached her to schedule a meeting, she would set it up to happen in her Magical Coffee Shop.

Soon, she held meetings there all the time! During our calls she would offhandedly say, "I had a meeting in my Magical Coffee Shop, and you'll never guess what happened..." (See what I mean about clients saying that?)

She *did* receive fantastic offers. Even better than what either of us could have predicted. She was promoted at work, and allowed to choose her own title. She was invited by outside organizations to speak at conferences and lead workshops on creativity and leadership in the U.S., Australia, and Europe, and was paid by her current employer to do it.

She keeps visiting her Magical Coffee Shop, because, as we both believe, there is more goodness coming her way. There must be! One latte can change your life. She proves that on a regular basis.

[HOMEWORK: ENJOY THE CRAP OUT OF YOUR LIFE]

- Are you delaying gratification? Acting like your own mean parent isn't very nice, and doesn't get you any closer to reaching your goals either. In fact, it's probably getting in your way. Grant yourself permission to enjoy yourself and do things you love every single day.

- What person or situation has you struggling right now? What you feel is valid. Honor all of your feelings, and look underneath to see what is really bothering you. It may not be who or what you thought it was.

- Why are you So Lucky that this struggle is happening? How is this an opportunity in disguise?

- Let the adorable, adventurous, creative Younger You lead. They know how you both can have more fun.

- Smile. Often. Right now, in fact.

CHAPTER 3

Do Things
You Haven't
Done Before

[DO THINGS YOU HAVEN'T DONE BEFORE]

Your younger self may already have pushed you out of your comfort zone. If so, you're well on your way to leaping.

Lesson 3 is to Do Things You Haven't Done Before.

This concept knows no bounds.

When I moved in the fall of 2013 to the rural town where I grew up two hours north of New York City in the Hudson Valley, the new friends I met invited me to join them for knitting classes, square-dancing hoedowns (seriously), and bouncing at a trampoline center.

I had not done any of these before, and as each new friend asked me to go with them I could feel a twinge of unease in the pit of my stomach. In the past, I would have taken that as a sign to reconsider their offers, perhaps waiting days to respond to their emails.

This time, I used that twinge as a sign I should not give it another thought, just say yes and show up.

I also took it as a sign not to tell anyone who would try to talk me out of it.

You have those people in your life. You love them dearly, but they remind you of Eeyore from *Winnie the Pooh*. The kinds of people who ask, "Are you sure you want to go for a walk on the beach? It might rain in four hours."

In the past, I used their warnings to talk myself out of things. Maybe you have too. In fact, I have sought them out when I was scared or nervous. Not engaging with them this time meant the twinge in my stomach went away on its own.

During each new experience I was awkward: I stepped on toes at the hoedown; unraveled half of the scarf I tried to knit; and in a truly spectacular display I fell face-first into a foam ball pit with my new friend and her two children watching. In these moments, my stomach seized up all over again. In each case I wondered if this was a bad idea and I should make an exit while no one was looking.

But again, I chose a different route. Instead of thinking about what was happening, I kept moving. Not one more thought before I took a deep breath, do-si-do-ed, drank water...anything to ensure my mind and body were occupied with a simple task. When I'm moving I'm not thinking or, in my case, over-thinking. There are plenty of places to think through a next step; a knitting class is not one of them, nor is a hoedown.

So I took a deep breath promenaded with my dance partner, kept knitting, and forced myself to laugh in the ball pit. As I did, I noticed that instead of being singled out – which is what fear and my Eeyore-like loved ones would have tried to convince me would happen – I was part of a circle of shared fun.

In each lesson of this book so far, I've asked you to notice how you feel in your body and mind about what's happening around you. How fear can lead you without you realizing it, for instance.

Now I want you to pay attention to what it feels like to do something out of your comfort zone, from having difficult conversations with someone you respect, to putting on ice skates for the first time in years.

Also notice, as in my case, how you use the people in your life to dictate what you do, so maybe you don't have to make a decision yourself. Who do you know who gives you permission to hold yourself back, and who encourages you to be bold? Be aware of how you feel around each of these people. When you choose to be different, you'll know who will be there to cheer you on. It helps to have company.

If you are skilled in fear facing and comfort-zone busting, hooray! If so, then it's time to kick it up a notch. What seems out of your comfort zone?

Remember how this relates to every part of your life, from scuba diving to saying "I love you" first. Take an honest look at what you have been seeking the courage to do: Carve out more time for yourself, ask for a raise, or travel on your own... What is a small step you can take? What's a big one?

There are several benefits to taking these steps. You see yourself stretch – and survive any stomach twinges – which may encourage you to do it again. It could bring you in contact with new people, who see you as a more spontaneous, braver version of who you think you are. They will assume you are that person, so much so, you may begin to believe them.

One more thought.

You've heard the phrase, "Fake it 'til you make it."

Many of us assume that faking it is bad, but it isn't if it gets you to try something you wouldn't have tried before. The truth is, you *are* that more vibrant, open, loving, fun person you hope you are. You need to see it and believe it. Try that person on for an afternoon, for a whole day, and then longer until it is a natural extension of you. Everyone starts somewhere.

[Sidebar: Adventure]

Years ago I had an argument with my coach, because he called me adventurous. I didn't take it as a compliment. I didn't even take a breath. I said, "No."

I knew adventurous people, and I was decidedly not one of them. I had a friend who traveled to Rio de Janeiro by herself, and didn't even book a hotel room in advance. When I asked her if she ever felt unsafe, she shrugged off my question and said she just didn't go out at night.

To this day, I have no idea how she did it. *She* is adventurous.

Undeterred, my coach said the word again. Adventurous. He gave the example of my trip to Vietnam. I thought about how scared I was when the plane landed, unable to read any signs or speak the language, surrounded by military officers holding rifles in the airport. Did I mention I had also lost our return tickets? When my husband and I finally made it to our hotel after being overcharged by the taxi driver, I cried, unsure how I would ever leave our room again.

Nope, adventurous people were like my friend. I needed to have my hotel booked and a guidebook in hand before I left, and I still cried. Nope, I was not adventurous.

It took the entire 45-minute coaching session for me to realize the word can have different meanings. I seemed adventurous to him, because he hadn't traveled to a non-English speaking country, something he was uncomfortable doing, just as my friend was adventurous to me because she did things beyond my comfort zone.

I could be cautiously adventurous if I wanted.

Looking back, this argument happened after I'd already taken a sabbatical, traveled to a bunch of countries, quit my job, attended art school, and started a business. It's laughable how hard I fought him over this one word.

You see where I'm going. As you tiptoe beyond your comfort zone, you might want to look a little further back at what got you to this moment. This is not your first leap. You've done things you thought you couldn't right up until the moment you did them. Other people have told you they admire you. They have said how they wish they could be like you.

Believe them.

If you're reading this book, you have already self-selected into a class of A-student overachievers and metaphoric mountain climbers. Pike's Peak may still be on the horizon, but I bet your friends and family have a running tally of other hills and schoolyard jungle gyms you've summited.

It's really important to not compare yourself with anyone else. This statement is true all of the time, and especially in the midst of a reinvention. Otherwise you will turn into someone who isn't you, and no one wants that.

Your goal is to become more *you* all the time.

Trial and error is a solid method to make this happen. Being scared and doing it anyway is another.

[CLIENT STORY: THE YELLOW KITCHEN WALL]

Years after working with one client, I still remember an image of her kitchen wall. I never saw it in person, but she told me about it over the phone when I asked her what she wanted.

"I don't know," she said.

She said those words often when we first began working together. She didn't know what she wanted as a career except not what she was doing at the time. She didn't know what to do about the guy she had been dating on and off for six years who had just told her he might want to get back together. She didn't know what she liked or whom she was meant to be or how to figure it out.

I asked her to remember a time when she knew what she wanted, and did it.

She said she didn't know. I was silent, allowing her thoughts to wander to what I hoped would be an anchor for the rest of our conversation.

"My kitchen wall," she finally blurted.

She had decided to paint her kitchen yellow, bought the paint, and did it.

I suggested she walk into her kitchen and look at the walls. From the other end of the phone, I could hear her moving through her apartment. When she stopped, I reminded her:

"You *do* know. These walls are proof."

Once we had the yellow wall, memories strung together of all of the other times when she knew what she wanted and did it. The time she quit smoking cold turkey, or when she moved cross-country to Boston despite her parents' concern.

If she had done those things, she could do even more now.

And she did. Her list of accomplishments is pretty impressive: leaving her teaching job, developing a freelance writing business, traveling by herself along the California coast to trace the steps of Jack Kerouac, and getting her MFA.

Whenever she was unsure of herself after that, she returned to the kitchen. Later we added her cat's meows to her reminders, each one an encouragement that what she wants is possible. I can speak from experience, he is a very talkative, supportive cat!

She doesn't tell me she doesn't know anymore. I wonder if she even remembers doing it, because that is the crazy-cool thing about becoming yourself. You can forget the part of you who was never really you anyway.

[HOMEWORK: DO THINGS YOU HAVEN'T DONE BEFORE]

- What have you been wanting the courage to do? What's one small step you can take, or a big one?

- How do you use the people in your life to give yourself courage, or hold yourself back? When you're unsure of doing something new, gravitate to the ones who will believe in you and tell the rest after you've done it.

- Try on a more vibrant, open, loving, fun version of yourself. Don't be afraid to fake it until you make it, just like all the high-achieving fear facers do!

- What does adventurous mean to you? See what has happened so far in your life and career to prove it's true.

- When was a time when you knew what you wanted, and did it? Write down your own kitchen wall story to remember how much you *do* know.

CHAPTER 4

Mind the
Gap

[MIND THE GAP]

When my clients are ready, incredible things happen. They have magical coffee, paint their kitchens, and create lives they love.

One day a client called into our session with this update:

"Remember how I imagined what it would be like to drive to my perfect job every morning? I was in the car yesterday, sipping my favorite tea, listening to my favorite music, and thinking about the day ahead, when I suddenly realized: 'This is *that* drive! It happened!'"

If you have been following along with the exercises in this book, it is likely you've had one of those moments. You are going about your normal routine

49

when suddenly... You hear yourself say something you wouldn't have said before. An opportunity comes your way you didn't think would be so easy. Someone repeats *the exact words* you just thought the other day when you were dreaming about what you wanted to happen. In a flash you realize it is working. The rest of your life can look different, because it already does right now.

When I hear about those moments, I want to jump up and down. You just discovered you're wearing those night vision goggles and are surrounded by gifts all with your name on them! Holy crap! Can you believe it?!

That feeling rocks. Let's have more of those.

What ensured my client would go on this perfect drive was her clarity.

She knew what she wanted, her ultimate goal.

She believed it was possible.

She imagined how it would feel when it happened.

Then she went on about her life with these tucked into her back pocket, and me checking in with her regularly to keep us focused.

[Those three things should be in your back pocket, too. If they aren't, give yourself a few minutes to get really clear. I'll be here when you get back.]

It had taken some time; by my notes from our conversations, she created the vision in March and went on that perfect drive in January the following year. Ten months. If I had told her back in March that it would take her ten months to make that vision a reality, it may have seemed like a long time. Now that it's here, it seems like no big deal.

That is what this lesson is about: What to do between when you get clear about your goal, and when it comes together.

The gap.

Lesson 4 is to Mind the Gap.

When you focus on the gap, it's like watching a cold teakettle heat up on the stove. The minutes stretch out seemingly forever.

The saying "Time flies when you're having fun" is also true. If you're loving life and doing things you've never done before, you don't focus as much on what hasn't happened yet. You enjoy the process. Then when you discover you're on the perfect drive to the perfect job you dreamed about, you will be delightfully surprised how it all came together so perfectly.

The gap also refers to when the going gets tough.

Like all superstars, you will have a quick and glorious win early on. New clients often call into our second and third sessions eager to tell me what happened. They didn't realize it would be this easy. It's working already. They like themselves and their lives more, and that feeling energizes them to push forward.

By the fifth call, I hear a different voice on the other end of the phone. They had another tough meeting with their boss, and all the good work we did is for naught. This one bad thing proves that what they want isn't going to happen. They are stuck in the mud.

Happens. Every. Time.

I am truly sorry about it, too. I know it's hard to see past a roadblock when it looked like the ride would be smooth from here on out.

But when you feel like giving up – telling yourself you wanted it too much, or didn't want it enough, or it wasn't meant to be – this is the moment instead to dig in your heels.

You don't have to see the way through; just keep going. The gap is about retrenching.

Feel yucky? Get out the glitter.

It's not working yet? Find a bright spot anywhere in your life and celebrate the crap out of it.

Want to give up? Tell yourself this setback is proof your goal will happen. [It's true.]

If you believe in God, the universe, fate, or signs, knowing that at some point on this path you will be challenged may help you stick with it. You are being asked how much you really want this. Can you face fear, failure, and discomfort? Yes? Good. Then you'll be rewarded for your fortitude. You've read enough stories and watched enough movies to know that's how it works.

No one said there wouldn't be bumps along the way. In fact, if you don't have them, you haven't set the bar high enough. Instead, you chose an easy goal, because you were afraid to say what you really wanted. Being scared, uncomfortable, and feeling the weight of the dream you've imagined means you really, really want this, and not getting it means something to you.

That makes you human for feeling, and superhuman for having the *chutzpa* to go for it. Bravo.

Your main job during this lesson is to notice when you reach the gap.

It may happen a few times along the way. Recognize when you arrive there, and pay attention to what you tell yourself.

Wanting to run away is normal. Actually running away isn't necessary. Treat yourself like you would a child on his first day of school. You know what he sees as a scary place with people he doesn't know is only scary because it's new to him. He'll be okay after he makes a friend or eats the yummy snack you packed for him. You can see past this moment in a way he can't. You understand his trepidation, and then gently walk him into the classroom.

Find a good friend, or be that big sister or parent you need to keep walking you forward.

Squeeze your hand, and tell yourself:

"I'm sorry that happened."

"I'm sorry it feels this way."

"You are so brave."

"It will get better, promise."

[SIDEBAR: DOODLES]

I've written about the gap before on my blog. This post is from 2012, and is just as true now. I love cheese doodles.

Five minutes from now

...the best thing ever is going to happen.

What if that's true? What if you're struggling right now, frustrated and disappointed things aren't working the way you want them to, but in five minutes all of it will change?

That would rock.

If it all turned around in five minutes, you'd be so busy celebrating you'd forget how it felt right before when it seemed like it-will-never-happen.

It's gonna happen. Maybe it will take 24 hours or a week or two years, but it will.

The big challenge then is: What do you do for the next four minutes and 59 seconds before it does?

I ask my clients, and myself, that often. How you handle yourself before what you want comes through is everything.

Think about what you really want. If it is already on its way, if it's assured it will happen, what will you do before it arrives?

Here's what I do:

Keep busy. I clean off my desk. Go through junk mail. Wash my dishes and clean the bathroom. I get small, easy items off my to-do list that will engross me for periods of time and help me feel accomplished.

Believe. Something amazing could happen five minutes from now. It makes me giddy with anticipation, and makes time pass.

Help someone else. Volunteer. Give a pep talk. Donate old clothes (see #1). It feels good. Those you help feel good, too.

Be grateful. Even before this new awesome thing arrives, life is pretty good. See how it is, and maybe send out a thank-you note or two (see #1).

Exercise. Make art. You know these work every time, you might as well do them.

Eat cheese doodles. I'm not above a little wallowing now and then.

Plan. Dude, this thing is about to happen. Maybe you should think about what you're going to do when it does! Make a new to-do list, buy yourself a new outfit, and write your acceptance speech.

Say yes. It might take less than five minutes. It might have been waiting in the wings for a while until you were ready. Well, be ready then! Open your arms up as wide as they can go.

If in five minutes what you want will arrive, what will you do?

[CLIENT STORY: SWEET LITTLE DOROTHY]

This client had already put herself in a good place when we began our work together. She liked her job and life in South Florida, but realized she might want to move back across the country to be closer to her family, especially her best friend's young daughter, Dorothy.

When she would say Dorothy's name, you could hear the smile in her voice. It was as if it conjured the girl's sweet little self right into the room.

One day, we were speaking on the phone while I was sitting in one of my favorite places in Washington, D.C.: The Willard Hotel. This place is transporting. High ceilings and marble columns mere steps from the White House. Abraham Lincoln held cabinet meetings there. Martin Luther King, Jr. practiced his "I Have a Dream" speech there the night before his address. I often walk out of my way to stroll through its hallway, or sit on a couch for an hour.

I was on a couch that day for our conversation, the fifth-call variety. She was unsure if things were working. What's more, she couldn't take another step. She had dutifully done all her coaching homework, pushing herself each week to research job postings in California, work her network, and envision the perfect scenario to speak to her boss...

She was completely overwhelmed. It came through loud and clear over the phone, and she worried if she felt this way because what she was doing wasn't working.

"It proves that it is," I said.

I told her just because she was too tired to do something didn't mean nothing was happening. For opportunities to fall into place, sometimes you have to take a breath and let them.

I asked if she could give herself permission to take time off from more to-dos. Her voice cracked. It was exactly what she wanted. Even more, she wanted to believe she didn't *have* to do anything else. Her relentless pace was too much to keep up with, but stopping had felt like giving up and she didn't want to do that.

The thought that things could happen even without her working hard felt like a huge sigh of relief.

We then brainstormed what would be relaxing and comforting, and would remind her that her goal was still very much in sight.

Her list included a massage, a nap, and taking herself out to dinner. How perfect we were talking about pampering while I was seated in such a beautiful spot. I sent her a photo of my view after we hung up.

A couple days later, she emailed an update. She felt better, more at ease, and hadn't realized how much having this permission meant to her.

"I just HAD to share this moment with you," she wrote. "My friend gave me this awesome gift of bath bombs and luxury bath melts. One of them was this funny looking blue ball with a rainbow on it...It wasn't until just a few moments ago when I read the description that came with these luxury bath bombs. You won't believe it, but the blue bath bomb with the rainbow is called, Dorothy!!! I just had to laugh. It's totally a sign and I feel so happy to get a message that I'm going in the right direction."

Guess where she lives now? Six months after our work together, she made moved home to California, with her boss happy to help her with the transition, and her family welcoming her back with open arms – including Dorothy.

[HOMEWORK: MIND THE GAP]

- Invent fun things to do during the gap between setting a goal and achieving it. Impromptu dance party, anyone?

- Listen to what you tell yourself in the tough moments. Give yourself the same tenderness and encouragement you would to a small child who feels unsure.

- Remind yourself this is all part of the plan. Every great adventure includes a few bumps. Keep your hands on the wheel and your foot on the pedal.

- Notice all that is already happening in your favor. Maybe not everything has fallen into place yet, but some has. If someone else were looking at your life, what would they see?

- Be generous with praise. You deserve it.

CHAPTER 5

Find Your Linchpin

[FIND YOUR LINCHPIN]

Okay, what the heck does this mean?

Let's start by getting out the dictionary.

In technical terms, a linchpin is a small instrument that keeps your car's tires in place on the end of an axle. Every piece of your car is doing its thing, and the linchpin holds it all together. You wouldn't drive without it.

Lesson 5 is to Find Your Linchpin.

The linchpins in your life are equally necessary for leaping and, as with your car, they can be so good at their jobs, you may not realize they're there.

Think of it this way...

So far you have the frame of a grand vision for your future, a few well-chosen steps to take, a greater appreciation of your current life, and a deeper understanding of what's been holding you back.

A solid linchpin added to all of that will propel you forward in a big way.

The clearest example I have of what one can do is from when I moved to Manhattan in 2000.

During my first few months, I floundered around like most transplants: figuring out my commute and finding the grocery store, the drycleaner and new friends. Then someone appeared in my life to utterly transform my experience. I met this linchpin while we were both visiting Boston for the weekend; we happened to end up at the same party, seated next to each other, and realized (coincidence upon coincidence!) we lived five blocks from each other back in Manhattan.

You can imagine how confounded I was at the time to have just bumped into this person, and now I can't fathom what my first years in Manhattan would have been like without her.

She had lived there longer than I had, and during our subsequent lunch – followed by meeting for weekend brunches and early morning workouts at the 92nd Street Y – she shared restaurant suggestions and doctor recommendations, and invited me to parties with her friends.

At the same time, another new friend introduced me to my spiritual self. I took a Reiki class she taught one weekend (doing something I hadn't done before, check!), and the moment she described the premise behind this healing, I found words to a belief I had held my whole life, but had never found words to express. All living things are made of energy, which means we are all connected and can send energy to heal one another. That felt true down deep inside of me, and I still believe it today.

A year later when this linchpin friend became a life coach, I was one of her first clients, working with her to build up the courage to ask my employer for a six-week sabbatical to travel Europe, and it happened! It was also she who would later tell me she thought I would make a good coach and encourage me to become one. She even performed the wedding to my first husband.

How much incredibleness can result from meeting just two people! There's even more I gained by knowing them and other linchpins through the years. I want to hug every one of them.

Who in your life appeared right when you needed them, even if you didn't know at the time how influential they would become?

These are the people who helped you settle into a new city, told you just what you needed to hear, or introduced you to the love your life. It may be the same with you as it was for me... The more I think about my leaps from the past, the more people I remember who were instrumental in making them successful, and the more gratitude I feel for the help that arrived right on time.

These are the people you are looking for now.

Part of this is magical or random depending on your point of view. What's great is that you don't have to do anything. Either way, magic or coincidence will conspire in your favor.

What you can do – and this is your assignment for this chapter – is to fine-tune your linchpin radar. Keep your mind, heart and eyes open. That way when this person arrives, you'll be ready.

You'll exclaim, "This is my linchpin!"

How do you fine-tune your radar?

You've already done some of the work by acknowledging linchpins of the past. Taking the extra step now to thank them, in your mind or in person, for the role they played in your life will help you welcome more in the future.

As you remember these special people, think back to how you found each other. The where-you-were's and who-said-what's, and especially how you acted in the moment to make the initial connection. If you don't normally talk to people in line at the supermarket but that day you did, it's an indication of what you might need to do now.

That's why a previous lesson is about doing something different. If you started that, who knows? You could already have met your next linchpin!

You must also notice your intuition and your body during this lesson, just as with the others. In the moments when you meet new people from here on out, pay attention to 1) your immediate, gut-check feeling about them, and 2) who they seem to be.

Are they so warm and kind you wonder if they could be for real? I've had a couple linchpins who have so eagerly welcomed me into their lives, I couldn't believe it. When I decided to trust who they showed me to be, everything started to fall into place.

I went along with their enthusiasm, because I, too, felt a spark of curiosity and connection with them.

In several instances upon shaking hands for the first time, I had the distinct thought that I would love to be this person's friend.

Pay attention to positive signs. This doesn't mean you need to co-sign a lease together, but you better keep in touch.

As you do, keep noticing how you feel and how these people show up. Is it still easy? Do they offer information that answers a question you just posed to yourself the day before?

Who knows when their instrumental role in your life may come about, but your awareness of their potential and your care in tending to these relationships must happen now.

[SIDEBAR: VACATION]

I am the friendliest person you can imagine on vacation. I say good morning to wait staff, groundskeepers, taxi drivers, and strangers in the elevator. I look them in the eye with a giant smile on my face.

I'm on vacation!

It's not that I'm typically unfriendly. I just go out of my way while on vacation because I feel like time has opened up. During a usual day, I sometimes won't acknowledge people next to me, even those who are trying to talk to me, because it feels as if the extra second it takes to give one cheerful nod will disturb my focus and set me back at work.

If you've ever sat next to me on an airplane while I was on a business trip, I'm sorry. There was a nice man from Chicago nine years ago who kept trying to say hello to me, and I kept ignoring him. Looking back, I wonder if he was the linchpin of all linchpins and I missed it.

I realized this about myself when I moved to Washington, D.C. from Manhattan in 2009. It was then I decided to try out being on vacation in my real life, too.

I still had deadlines and clients. I still found myself rushing to networking events and business meetings. The only difference was that whenever I walked somewhere, I would look up.

I thanked people who held the door open. In fact, I held the door open for others more often. I smiled at checkout people and complimented bank tellers on their earrings.

Being friendly isn't a new concept, I realize. Perhaps you are already more adept at it than me.

Something special happens when other people feel seen. I've mentioned magical happenstances a couple times in this book, and this is definitely an opportunity for such an experience.

When someone feels seen, listened to, appreciated, and acknowledged, they are more likely to see, listen to, appreciate, and acknowledge you. As a result, both of you will come away from the exchange with a brighter outlook.

On the most basic level, that just makes your life better on a daily basis. On any other level, you're manifesting the best outcome in every situation with less work required. Or, no work at all.

If you are actively connecting with the world around you, more and more connections will find their way to you.

Don't wait to go on a vacation. Start right now.

...

A few caveats about the linchpin. It may take a while to notice which person you meet opens everything else up, or for their linchpin status to materialize. In D.C., for instance, it took me nine months to meet my linchpin – well, the big one, anyway, who singlehandedly introduced me to all my closest friends and inspired me to try public speaking for the first time. Holy changing my whole life!

I'm positive there were other smaller linchpins in D.C., too. In fact, I just remembered one! There was a woman to whom I provided a sample coaching session. At the end of the call she said, "You're new in town, do you need any recommendations?" She suggested several great doctors on the spot, and since then has sent me several clients through the years, and we have never met in person!

What speeds along the process is the stuff you can control – your vacation mindset and your linchpin radar.

A second caveat: There isn't just one linchpin. There are dozens, if not more. This is really about your radar.

When you welcome assistance from anywhere and everywhere, your big goals happen faster, better, easier. If you want to make this hard on yourself, believing that if you don't work at it you don't deserve your goal, that's your choice. I'm telling you it just isn't true.

Instead, decide right now to believe something more generous about opportunities knocking on your door, or walking into your magical coffee shop. Sure, you'll do the work to sit in the coffee shop, keeping your eyes and ears perked for perfectly timed opportunities to arrive. But, it doesn't have to be hard. In fact, it won't be if you believe another way is possible.

[CLIENT STORY: JUST WHAT I NEEDED TO HEAR]

In my first year of coaching, I launched a six-week program called Mommy Drama to provide women with a safe space to explore whether they wanted to become mothers. It's a gift that we have a choice in our society, but that doesn't make it easier to know or feel confident about the answer. Getting past what you think you *should* do, and what others think you should do, gets enormously easier when you're surrounded by other women right where you are. You get to hear your own voice.

That's what I needed at the time, as a professional woman who defined herself by her career and was afraid she might lose that in the process of putting a child's needs first. I didn't feel like I could talk to my friends or family who had already made their choices and assumed I would choose the same. On more than one occasion I wondered if I was the only one who didn't know if she wanted to be a mom.

When I started the program, though, women came forward, grateful they had somewhere they could share how confused and anxious they were about this life-altering decision.

One was a great friend of mine. She and I had confided in each other about our apprehension, and those conversations were the impetus for me to create Mommy Drama. When I announced the program, she immediately signed up.

Of everyone there, my friend was the most vocal about her struggle. Each week, the group discussions and homework assignments pushed her, and everyone, to look hard at what this choice really meant. We unearthed a lot of demons.

Still, she wasn't sure. By the third call with everyone, I think she and I both wondered whether she'd be able to come to a decision by the end.

And then something happened. Another woman in the group, a skilled coach navigating the decision for herself, heard something in my friend's distress and named it out loud. Everyone in our virtual room could hear a shift in her voice, the tears caught in her throat, and the nerve finally touched.

The two spoke separately afterward, and the next time we all gathered, it was as if my friend was a different person. She was a more vulnerable version of herself. The decision shone out of her.

I feel privileged to know and love the little girl she and her husband welcomed into their lives a couple years later.

As a coach and her friend, part of me wanted to be her linchpin. Even more profound, though, was to witness someone being in the right place at the right time to hear what they need to hear.

[HOMEWORK: FIND YOUR LINCHPIN]

- Remember the linchpins of your past. Send them a mental or real thank-you note. Even if you haven't spoken in a decade, it's worth it.

- Hone your linchpin radar. Expect these people to find you, and feel in advance how terrific it will be when they do. Then look for them everywhere.

- Notice who and what you are drawn to, and how easily they fit into the vision of your great life. Give priority to these natural connections.

- Vacation mind! You always, always have time to smile.

- Bonus: Witnessing someone else finding their linchpin is a sign yours is right around the corner.

CHAPTER 6

See What
We Did
There?

[SEE WHAT WE DID THERE?]

You are cruising!!

Do you feel it? Hopefully things have been falling perfectly into place as you enjoy the crap out of everything in sight.

This is the moment to reflect back on your progress. See what you made happen. Well, not just see it, but write it down. Remember the order of events, and understand why it worked.

Lesson 6 is to See What We Did There.

After you finish this book, there will be many more leaps in your future. You love life too much to stop here. We're getting you over a big hump with these lessons, and from your new vantage point you'll see more you want to discover.

Taking stock now creates a template for how to do it again.

Take five minutes to write down what has happened since beginning these lessons. Little things count. In fact, little things pave the way for big things, so without those you wouldn't be here.

For example: Maybe there was a person you bumped into who told you about a book you needed to read, and reading it lead you to ask your boss for a raise.

Write down who the person was, the scenario in which you bumped into each other, the passage in the book with the most meaning, and the fact that you got a raise. YAY, by the way. High five.

In addition, write down what made each of those things work well. What you were doing and how were you acting when you bumped into this person? What did you say that prompted them to recommend the book? Why was now the right time for you to read it? What made this conversation with your boss feel different than others?

This is not just about the end game; I hope that's obvious by now. This is about understanding who you are and what reinvention uniquely looks like for you, so you can repeat it.

Our society has a nasty habit of achieving goals and moving on. What's next? What's next? What's next?

One of the benefits of coaching is the time for reflection. We analyze what you accomplished from every angle – specifically looking for what was it about *you* that made it possible.

Some clients cringe about this part. "Tough tooties," as my mom would say. *You* climbed this mountain. Yes, you had help, but you decided to climb it now, in this way. *You* recognized opportunities as they arose, and *you* seized them.

I want you to stick with Lesson 6 for at least 24 hours. A week would be even better. I'm serious.

This is just like how celebrating the crap out of your current life prepares you for loving the crap out of where you land after your big leap. If you keep moving now, what you will have is a list of accolades (you probably already do), but no real sense of accomplishment. No deep understanding of how much you are capable of. A list doesn't give you that; reflection does.

If you're getting antsy, think about this from the point of view of a favorite person in your life. If they just did what you did, you would probably throw them a party with streamers, confetti, and a glass of champagne.

You get permission to be proud of yourself. It's a good thing, no matter what you've been told in the past. Many of us carry around beliefs that celebrating is selfish. Learning to enjoy your life more in Lesson 5 was preparing you for this moment. Savor what *you did*. No one else needs to give you permission to do that, except for you.

Climbing off my soapbox to continue the dance party… You did it! Woo! You did this wonderful thing you didn't think was possible. Not only did you prove it is indeed possible, but it is happening, right now, to you.

How do you feel?

Notice how your body reacts to achieving a milestone. Where do you feel it? Does it have a sensation, a color, or a sound? What image comes to mind?

In addition to developing your ability to celebrate, you have also been growing in self-awareness.

Your feelings get added to the template you are creating of how leaps work for you. This information lets you know what it's like when you achieve something, so when you start this book again with a new goal (I hope you will), you'll really know what you're aiming for: This feeling.

That was the reflection portion of the lesson; time for celebration. No, we're not done!

Answer without another thought: What feels like a total indulgence? What would be fun to do, maybe something you haven't done in a long time?

Now, I want you to make a second list. Write down at least five things that would unequivocally make your day.

Choose at least one, preferably all five, to do this week in order to celebrate your achievement. If going to Costa Rica is on the list, and you're about to tell me you can't afford it yet or offer up some other excuse, I want you to look at flights to Costa Rica, put a date on your calendar when you'll go – even a year from now – and then do something that represents this trip in the next couple days. Flip through a travel book on the country. Go to a local restaurant that serves food from there. Buy little umbrellas for all your drinks, because that's the one of things you like about staying at a resort.

You get the idea.

Now, do it.

One more thing: While you're celebrating, I want you to tell yourself why. "I am proud of myself for getting this raise. Cheers to me!"

If it feels awkward, say it anyway. If it makes you giggle, say it a second time.

You know how good it feels to hear praise from someone you respect? We're giving you that. Other people are proud of you, too. It would be fantastic to share your good news with them. And acknowledging yourself out loud is the extra special gold star on top of enjoying the crap out of things.

You made it.

[SIDEBAR: WHY]

By now, you may be asking yourself, "But where is the plan?"

That's valid. The A-students among us may notice right away that at no point have I offered a list of actions to get you from point A to B. Well I have, but likely they look different from the plan you had in mind.

That's because you are fully capable of doing that yourself. You know very well how to create and check things off a to-do list.

All my clients do. You're reading this, because you didn't exactly know what you were meant to be doing (yet), or you knew and you hadn't figured out how to get there (yet).

The solution for either is not to figure it out.

Most of us get stuck in our heads trying to figure out *everything*.

This deserves a disclaimer like the ones at the end of drug commercials:

WARNING: *Trying to "figure it out" may cause headaches, dizziness, nausea, vomiting, loose stool (love that one), loss of sleep, loss of appetite, elevated heart rate, and talking yourself in circles.*

You can do all of that on your own time. This was, and is, about changing your perspective. Liking yourself more. Learning to turn challenges into opportunities. Making the most out of what's right in front of you – the reason behind every item you put on your to-do list. The "why."

Your "why" is your North Star. When you have consciously and carefully chosen it, everything else aligns, or as I like to think about it: When you are doing what you're supposed to be doing, the universe conspires on your behalf in delightfully unexpected ways.

You enjoy life more, hopefully like you do now. And then, the to-do's (gasp!) don't matter as much.

If you have been a to-do lover all your life, and just noticed you haven't been paying as much attention to them, this is it! Ding ding ding! Willy Wonka is handing you the keys to the chocolate factory.

If, on the other hand, you are worried you don't have a plan, or maybe your goal isn't good enough or happening fast enough, that's just fear waving hello. Somehow it made its way into the driver's seat for this turn around the block.

Luckily you control the traffic in this town, so put up a stop sign and kindly ask fear to wait for the bus.

[CLIENT STORY: HOLY MOLY MATRIMONY]

Remember the client from the first chapter, the one who set her sights on being calm and confident by age 40, and then proceeded to leap like nobody's business?

She had already reached a good place in her life. She liked her job more; enjoyed rock climbing and orienteering outside the office; knew her divorce, while difficult, was the right decision; and was open to dating though not dependent on it.

The same month as her 39th birthday, I held a special conference call with eight of my most successful clients, many of them featured in this book. Over the years, they had changed how they saw themselves and what they believed was possible, which in turn changed nearly their entire lives. If they could do that on their own and in our one-on-one calls together, what could happen if they all helped manifest each other's dream goals?

You know how an idea gains momentum when more people are behind it, and then is more likely to happen? These elite clients joining forces in a series of monthly calls for one year offered the possibility of exponential growth for them as individuals and for the group as a whole.

That's exactly what happened.

The first call in our "virtual living room of collective magic" as one of them called it, took place in January. I had them close their eyes and visualize each month of the coming year, everything they thought would happen and wished for, right up to the following New Year's Eve.

After that, they introduced themselves. Most of these clients didn't know each other, living in cities across the country and around the world. Everyone was beginning with a clean slate. How they introduced themselves and what they said they wanted for the year ahead was all anyone else would know about them.

It made it easier to believe anything and everything was possible for them.

When it was this client's turn to introduce herself and her dream for the year ahead, she lived up to the bright-eyed and open-hearted person I had come to know and love.

She said, "By next January, I'll be engaged and pregnant."

My mouth gaped open on the other end of the phone. More than her being single and not even on a dating site at the time, and her having been on the fence about having children for the nine years we'd known each other, was my utter shock at what I was witnessing. Because of the premise and promise of this gathering – that more is possible than we can ever imagine if we believe it and if others believe in it too – she didn't hold back.

In fact, in stepping forward with this bold pronouncement she challenged everyone else in our virtual living room, myself included, to step up with her.

I composed myself simply with, "That's awesome, and can totally happen!"

It wasn't a throwaway comment by the way. We don't need to know how something is going to happen in order for it to come to be. We just need to believe, or try our best to, and take any step in front of us. Not the *right* step, but any step. Keep moving and things conspire on your behalf.

So though I was surprised, to say the least, I trusted in her and in the power of our beliefs. Others on the call followed with their support, and shared their dreams and goals for the year ahead. We continued to gather on the phone once a month after that, as well as on email and Facebook in between.

Fast forward twelve months. I can hardly believe it. One year later from when she made this statement, she was wearing the most beautiful diamond ring. A man she'd met a year prior through friends and then hadn't seen again, had resurfaced a few months before and from the moment they began dating it just felt right.

By February? You guessed it. She was pregnant!

Recently she and her husband welcomed their son, a bundle of collective magic.

She did this. We held the space for her in our virtual living room, and she created this incredibly full life for herself.

I'm immensely proud of her...and even better, she is proud of herself!

[HOMEWORK: SEE WHAT WE DID THERE?]

- What has happened since starting this book? What have you learned, done differently, what things have fallen into place? Capture them all.

- What you were doing and how were you acting in order for these things to fall into place? Remember this is about understanding who you are and what reinvention uniquely looks like for you, so you can repeat it.

- Write down five things that would unequivocally make your day. Give them to yourself. You deserve it.

- Notice if fear is driving, and have it take the bus.

- Be proud of yourself. Repeat: "I did this. I did this. How cool am I?" (Answer: Very.)

CHAPTER 7

In Case of Emergency, Break Glass

[IN CASE OF EMERGENCY, BREAK GLASS]

We made it.

You're here, because like Willy Wonka's young friend, Charlie, you stuck with it; kept your wits, wonder, and self-awareness about you throughout; and are ready to experience the chocolate-covered fruits of your labor. (Speaking of which, I hope you had a sweet treat as part of your celebration in Lesson 6.)

Now, we're on to what's required to make sure you keep leaping with ease.

Lesson 7 is In Case of Emergency, Break Glass.

You started some of that work earlier by writing down what your role has been in making your goals possible. If you have been putting off that writing assignment, by the way, now is the moment to get to it.

Have a go, even if you completed the writing assignment already. This is a good refresher. Jot down what has worked so far, how it worked out, and what your role was in making it happen.

I'll wait.

Take your time.

I'll be here dancing in the meantime… *"sha lala lala lala lala lala ti da. Just like that."*

(Van Morrison, if you couldn't tell.)

That wasn't so hard was it? It's a wonder what you accomplish when you sit down for a couple minutes.

Onward.

We are building your leap template. The notes above and from Lesson 6 are the foundation. You have collected invaluable information about what works for you, and what doesn't. When organized together, you can walk yourself through the process whenever you need it in the future.

The number one question to ask yourself: What did you learn from your latest success that you want to remember for next time?

I pose this question to clients as they are ending a year, a job, or a relationship. Before you can truly move on, you need to decide what you want to leave behind and what you want to take with you.

I could share my own lessons from our time together, but they won't mean as much. When the poop really hits the proverbial fan, your own words will best remind you how resourceful and capable you really are.

This is the emergency container, like the one you see behind glass in office buildings and on buses. Your words will be your fire extinguisher.

Other questions to consider:

If you could have known something before your last leap, what would have been most helpful?

What made now the perfect time to make this leap? How did you know?

What kind of signs, symbols, milestones or forcing mechanisms helped you know you were doing the right thing and were ready to go for it?

What is most helpful to you when you're feeling energized and want to keep feeling that way? How about when you're flailing and need a pep talk? What makes these actions you take or people you speak to so helpful?

Where do you do your best work? (In an office, out in nature, in the company of creative minds...)

What do you want to NEVER FORGET? (About yourself, about what it takes to get over a major roadblock, about the exhilaration of conquering a fear...)

The answers to these are your Leap Template to summit any mountain in the future.

[SIDEBAR: RE-MEMORIES]

The last call with clients is always bittersweet. We've talked about real, sometimes vulnerable, things in our time together.

Our coaching relationship's solid foundation of respect, honesty, and commitment was established on our first call. It was then we decided our markers for success so we both would know when we reached them, and we discussed what each of us needed from the other in order to do our best work. It's the kind of conversation every relationship would benefit from, even with friends and loved ones.

Our final session is the bookend to that. We review what there is to celebrate, and say what we need to say to one another in order to feel complete.

Finally, we talk about what comes next. Endings aren't static things. The past is always accessible whenever you need to refer back to it. Clients share where they see themselves headed, and what valuable lessons they want to take with them.

I also ask how they want me to think about them, because our relationship isn't really over. I'm still here believing in you long after our calls end or this book is put away, and that's powerful stuff.

While speaking with a client about what she had achieved during our time together, she was on an absolute high. She had started a business making healthy, grain-free goodies, and we had worked together until she was clear on what her business was, narrowing down all her interests so that she could focus on immediate sales in the short term. By our last call, she had perfected a couple key recipes, received her first orders, and felt more confident in her capabilities.

We talked about how she would celebrate these accomplishments in order to stoke the fire for more in the future. Then I asked her what tips and words of wisdom she wanted to hold onto in case she hit a snag in the future. Reminders & Memories, or Re-Memories so to speak.

She began listing them out loud, her excitement and pride increasing with every addition. She had a lot!

After the call, I emailed my notes of her in-case-of-emergency reminders, so she could post them somewhere she would always see them.

She replied that she had decorated a box, writing each on a strip of paper and adding a few meaningful quotes to the mix. Whenever she needed an extra boost, she could pull one out of the box and receive a pep talk to keep going, she knows what's she doing, and things will work out for the best.

...

It can be so easy to celebrate a win and move onto what's next without any thought about the down swing that surely will come at some point.

Downswings are good, by the way.

They happen because you continue to leap your adventurous self into new, uncomfortable territory. It will be worth it, just as it was this time, but when discomfort strikes you can forget you have been here before.

Next time discomfort, vulnerability or fear rear their heads, congratulate yourself. Feeling fear proves you really want what you're going after. If you aren't afraid, you're being safe. Remember successful people face the unfamiliar on a regular basis – what distinguishes them is that when others might turn back, they dig in their heels and stick with it. We both know I'm talking about you.

When you're on a high after a win, that's the time to take notes. So spend a few minutes now to build your own list of reminders and lessons learned based on the questions above.

Write those puppies down and put them in a special place for when you need them the most. Your own Re-Memory box, bulletin board, list on your phone, or folder on your desktop.

Your future self, and I, will thank you for doing this.

[CLIENT STORY: HOLDING STEADY]

How lucky are you? You get TWO client stories in this chapter.

This second client is one of a kind. Smart, driven, with a voracious appetite for learning new things and advocating for beleaguered communities around the world.

He was an executive in a large technology firm when we started working together, and was really happy there. He liked his colleagues and bosses, and the resources and benefits a large organization afforded him.

Still, he had an inkling another career would make him even more fulfilled. He didn't know yet what it was, but he put loads of faith in us figuring it out.

He fully embraced the research stage – imagining his ideal life and work, and exploring what could get him there. He was still immersed in it when he received news he would be one of thousands of people chosen for a round of layoffs.

Like a champ, he embraced that as well. He told me he had considered if he should be upset about it, or feel like his ego was bruised, but then decided the answer was no. He had already been thinking about a change, and actively pursuing it through our work, so he felt organized and encouraged. He would continue to put his energy there.

When we checked in on his progress a few calls later, he relayed the inspiring coffees and informational interviews he was having on a near-daily basis. He enjoyed it so much, he said, he wanted to stay with this for a while.

Here was a client who was pro-actively standing still. He recognized this moment in his life was the closest he had ever been to the ideal one we imagined when we first began.

Right this minute, he was looking for work, carefully watching his finances, and following his plan to rate opportunities by how they fit into each of his criteria (he even had a spreadsheet, bless him). He was working out every day, going to yoga, and journaling with intention. He loved all of it. He wanted to hang there for a while, soak it in, and make sure he felt equally enamored with the next job he chose.

You can decide to be happy with where you are while being open to what's next. If you glean nothing else from his story and this book, I hope it's this.

[HOMEWORK: IN CASE OF EMERGENCY, BREAK GLASS]

- What did you learn from your current leap that you want to remember for next time?

- What made now the perfect time to make this leap? How did you know?

- What helps you know you're doing the right thing and that you should keep going – perhaps in the form of signs or gut feelings?

- Design a Re-Memory box to store your favorite reminders. A place you'll see regularly, such as a bulletin board over your desk or file on your computer, so you can return to it often.

Epilogue

[Epilogue]

You came to this book because good-enough wasn't good-enough anymore, and I hope in the span of our time you discovered your life is more amazing than you ever imagined and how much is truly possible when you believe it is.

It just keeps getting better from here.

Cue the sparkles, sprinkles, champagne, and Stevie Wonder.

Lauree Ostrofsky helps people love their lives, work and each other more every day. She lives in her childhood home in New York's Hudson Valley and looks forward to daily visits from a little black stray cat named Butterfly. This is her second book; her first is entitled, *I'm scared & doing it anyway.*

Learn more about her writing, coaching and hugging at www.simplyleap.com.

[ACKNOWLEDGEMENTS]

Top billing in the thanks department goes to YOU. It means more than I can express to share stories, and have you read them and share your stories in return. May this book continue our conversations.

Heartfelt appreciation for the editors and friends who guided this book into being, especially Robin Flanigan, and also Emma Flynn, David Hicks, Amanda Hirsch, and Rebecca Nolen.

Thank you to Ching-Hua, Christine, James, Katy, Monique, Monique (there were two!), and Stephanie for allowing me to witness your transformations and offer them here. Your daring fear-facing and infectious joy inspire everyone around you. We are all so lucky.

Thank you to family and friends for your encouraging hugs, wise counsel and sparkle-tastic playfulness. I wouldn't be here, with this book and in this stage of my life, without you: Mom, Dad, Bea, Kerry Jo, Robin, Jeanne, Nadine, Jill, Angelique, Amy, Jan, Janne, and the Small Business Women & Wine, Hudson Valley Women in Business, and Life-Lovers & Simply Leapers communities.

Finally, I'm grateful for every positive sign along the way. The burst of sunshine through the window while writing, the brightly-colored leaf waving on an otherwise still tree during a morning walk, and inspiration kicking in at perfect moments. It feels so good to know I'm where I'm meant to be, doing what I'm meant to do. Signs received. Thanks.

Much love from me to all of you.

Made in the USA
San Bernardino, CA
09 August 2017